Embers

Logan Deadmond

BookLeaf
Publishing
India | USA | UK

Presentation by *BookLeaf Publishing*

Web: www.bookleafpub.com

E-mail: info@bookleafpub.com

ISBN: 9789358317831

First edition 2023

DEDICATION

To Camryn and Kate, my loves. And to Ed, the great mountain man who inspired me to write these sorts of things

PREFACE

Grab a cup of coffee or tea, a glass of wine or whiskey, find a quiet place to read and find a few of these that you like. If you feel compelled to, feel free to let me know all about what your favorites are and why. In any case, I sincerely hope you enjoy what you find here.

#1

Decide who you'll be on that singular day

Your exploits, your triumphs, and write down
the way
-
Then tear the sheet up weeks later, grab another

Make a new you just in time for the summer
-
And when that you inevitably fades

Blown away by distractions, lost to the haze
-
Pick up that old pen you tossed back in May

Have the courage to look in the mirror and say:
-
"The you that's been you-ing this way is no
longer.

The you that will you from now on will you
stronger."
-
For fortune, good health, some powerful reason,

You'll dream up a you for the colder season
-

And when it comes near, that familiar date,

You'll try to claw back the time and yell "wait!"
-

You might look at the you that you are,
dismayed,

But look, dear you, at the progress you made
-

Notch the losses, the wins, the memories and
then,

Find the wit and the nerve to write a new you
again

#2

I've got to go the sun is up there's just no time to
waste

To go consume the world's array with nothing
short of haste

I've got to go to run the circles faster, faster still

To catch the day's distractions from the great
distraction mill

I've got to go I've got to go the moment's not
enough

I've got to go I've got to go, to fake, to fill, to
fluff

I've got to go I've got to go I've got to get there
fast

I've got to go I've got to go this wasn't built to
last

I've got to go I've got to go I've got to go again

I've got to go I've got to go I've got to go but
when

I've got to go I've got to go…

#3

5

Among the thieves,
roll up your sleeves

#4

Take a risk and make the choice
or face head-on you've lost your voice

Infinite

And the firm hand that reaches down
unwavering and unquestioning to pull you up
again, again, again. Again.

And the warmth of toasted bread

And the slow-moving tide of everything passing
back and forth between you

And the hills climbed

And the hills not climbed

And the rest of it all

#6

The fire grows hotter grows higher grows
brighter.
Gather round, let your spirit grow lighter.

The restless awe and clamor for more.
The wise, their rumblings will ignore.

For what they forget that the wise remembers.
Is that life is sustained and maintained by the
embers.

October's Promise

Fear the fables, or their author?
It's all but fiction. Shouldn't bother
But you know and know it well
The haunts ring a familiar bell

Feel the fear and know it's reason
Dance with devils real this season
And when you waltz with wicked guests
Something stirs within your chest

From the depths and from the heights
Frights and frights and frights and frights
Turn about your restless mind
Worry now, what might you find?

~

Wayward, winding, wandering through
The fog of mind, the vice like glue
Off the road and into the ditch
Guided by the shimmering witch

~

~

Tools not toys, or so you thought
Until you find out what you've wrought

You'll see theyve owned you all this while
Entranced you with vampiric guile
~

~

Aimed to settle, aimed to please
Died distressed on tired knees
Alive again, but then what for?
Best find something. Something more.
~

~

Could be this world or the next
Not sure where the road connects
Just that once it wasn't so
Not so very long ago
~

More important than what you find
Is what you're able to leave behind
Take new hope. Move forth. Believe.
And come back next All Hallows' Eve

#8

I'll walk the tightrope
but don't ever say that I played a single game to
lose

I'll carry the boulders
but when I go out, I'll go out the way that I
choose

I'll paddle upstream
but not for it to seem like I'm more than
just a person like you

I'll climb up the mountain
in the end just to find that the trek
was worth more than the view

#9

Measure out the dosage right
Equal portions, fight and flight
Down the hatch and off you go
Dreams the only thing in tow

Infinite pt. 2

I saw feet that belonged on grass in summertime

I saw a forehead furrowed with wonder and
fervor for all the little big things the world has to
offer

I saw hands that would search and grab too
firmly the entire future and the blanket at night

I saw eyes looking through me that belonged to
the both of us

If the world ever tilted too far on its axis I had a
sworn oath in me to set it right

What a difference it can make in a day, to know
to whom you'll say that sweet "goodnight"

#11

Strawberry red and blood orange burst into
streaks in a black ocean above.

The water below was in a mood to play around
with the reflecting light as if to show it was able
to do a wonderful and simple set of magic tricks
when given the chance.

To purple then to blue and it became impossible
to tell if it was the stillness and quiet of the
world behind the windshield bathed in the
colorful display, or the presence of the angel
resting at arm's reach that gave the night all of
it's mythical qualities.

July would never again seem so new.

#12

15

Widely adored, with great fanfare received!
But answer to the mirror: were you or them
deceived?

#13

Scant rations left for the closed-minded at the
table of life. Hold fast to only what you know
and count yourself among the hungry. Better to
eat, drink, find fulfillment and company beyond
the brief discomfort of the unknown.

#14

After years of exploration in the Goldilocks zone

The galaxy explorers found a viable new home

A blue-green oasis in a panoply of stars

New life, new hope, for a future that could be
ours

The old world abandoned, depleted, neglected

Catastrophes that somehow no one expected

Now to our new future this world would give
birth

Until we found others on this place they call
Earth

Across the universe we'd traveled to find

That we weren't, after all, one-of-a-kind

The first and the worst new discovery made

Left every last one of us deeply dismayed

The residents here, these neighbors of Mars

Were looking for new worlds out in the stars

They'd ruined this Eden at a rapid rate

And would suffer the same tragic, human fate

< Tomorrow

Do we know enough to know we don't know
enough ?

Not yet

Do we have the courage to cast off the veils ?

Not yet

Are we brave enough to trade off want for need
in all the ways that matter ?

Not yet

And yet…

Runner's Drumbeat

Step
Excitement
Step
Focus
Step
Steady
Step
Maintain
Step
Breathe
Step
Pain
Step
Demons
Step
Breakthrough
Step
Onward
Step
Fight
Step
Fight
Step
Finish

Step
Elation

There's A Park I Know

There's a park I know where you can
swing off the edge of the earth dangling
your feet over space and time and
everything. You can't walk there or drive a car
to get to it. Well you can, but you see, that's not
really the point. I can tell you about it sometime.

For Ed

I dreamt I roamed the mountains
And breathed that crisp, cool air

I dreamt I walked by riverside to
see what I'd find there

I dreamt the dream as night was falling
Somehow, somewhere…Fires Creek calling…

I didn't know just what it meant
And several days and nights I spent

Thinking of that ethereal call
And where it came from after all

I woke abruptly out of bed
To find the dream that filled my head

Was given on purpose, in the end
By a kind, wise man I call a friend

I met him only once or twice
But those moments would suffice

For that old man out in those hills,

Removed from shallow, cheap new thrills

Passed along a lifelong gift
To set at night my mind adrift

To quiet streams and peaceful days
To set my wandering heart ablaze

For that gift it must be said,
A solemn "thank you", to my friend Ed

#19

The ground flows like the sea and sifts through
the hands here
Horizon to horizon a golden ocean

I've lost track of days and nights and all time
here
Just hazy and nonstop and forward motion

I'll get to the end with this strange-looking
horse. I'll endure. I'll persevere.

My footprints erased, this letter I've written, all
to ever prove I was here

#20

And should we go, let us not take here there. For there wouldn't have been a purpose to go, if so

#21

Goodnight to the silent void
Says the drifting asteroid
If I were a comet, of all things
I'd lie to rest in Saturn's rings